Till We Meet Again

A memories book for recording the precious lives of stillborn babies...gone too soon

Tarlia Bartsch

Published by: Tarlia Bartsch
Author Email: till-we-meet-again@outlook.com
Facebook: https://www.facebook.com/till.we.meet.again.memorybook
Website: www.tillwemeetagainmemorybook.com.au

Back Cover Photograph
Liquidart Photos
Email: liquidartphotos@bigpond.com

Cover and internal image design
City Signs and Print
Email: citysigns@internode.on.net

National Library of Australia Cataloguing-in-Publication entry
Author: Bartsch, Tarlia L., 1983- author.
Title: Till we meet again : a memories book for recording the
              precious lives of stillborn babies
              ...... gone too soon / Tarlia Bartsch ;
              edited by Mary R Gudzenovs.
ISBN: 9780994153227 (hardback)
Subjects: Bartsch, Tarlia L., 1983-
              Stillbirth.
              Infants--Death.
              Bereavement.
Other Authors/Contributors:
              Gudzenovs, Mary R., editor.
Dewey Number: 155.937085

In memory of

Jayden Tate Bartsch
Born still on the 19th December 2011

&

Grace Langmaid
Born still on the 27th May 2005

Grace, your amazing mum was a rock of support,
whose knowledge, love and infectious laugh helped me through.

Two precious angels playing together in heaven.

This Book belongs to

_____

with love from

_____

One tiny little baby boy...

Counting all ten fingers, and ten teeny tiny toes.
One little dinky mouth and lips, and a precious button nose.
One little balding head, which soon would sport your hair.
All neatly knitted together, with such love and such care.

Ten tiny little fingers, that will never touch my face.
Ane ten teeny tiny toes, that will never walk or chase.
One little dinky mouth and lips, that will never say my name.
One little balding head so sweet, such a delicate, dear frame.

One tiny little baby silent and still, but sobs they echo through.
A mum and dad are broken, daunted by the life they face without you.
No trips down to the beach to play, no gel to spike your hair.
No teaching words while awe abounds, as you sit and simply stare.
No putting you in your car seat, an adventure to be had.
No cuddles with your mummy, no football with your dad.

Instead we have just hours, to make memories with you.
Take photos, pick a name we love, and say goodbye too...
An ache that's felt forever, a piece gone from our heart.
And moving on with life each day. Where really do we start?
An empty cot, an empty room, a silence tinged with pain.
Of a precious little baby boy, we'll never hold again.

Written by Tarlia Bartsch
For Jayden Tate Bartsch , 19th December 2011

Contents

'I held you, I breathed you in. Your smell, your baby soft skin.

Your silent birth awakened feelings from my inner core.

I have known no deeper pain and there can be no higher love.'

~Nicola Connors~

Introduction

My name is Tarlia Bartsch. I'm the proud mum of three boys. Two of my boys walk closely by my side, one I hold in my heart.

I found out I was pregnant for the second time in early 2011. But this time was different. I knew what I was in for, the pain, the sickness, the anxiety and depression, and after three years of severe pain and surgeries from my first child's birth, I was terrified. After a few weeks the anxiety settled and I began to get excited that I was going to be a mum again. This time it would be different, this time would be a healing experience and I would be so blessed to have that second baby I never thought I would have.

I remember at sixteen weeks pregnant, laying on my bed and watching my tummy roll as our little acrobat showed off his skills. My first born came over and placed his ear on my tummy and began to giggle as he said 'the baby is kicking my ear'. Our baby wasn't even born yet and already he was interacting with his big brother. It was such a beautiful moment, one I will forever treasure. I was so happy. Glowing, as my tummy started to pop out for the world to see. We received congratulations from everywhere for the baby we said we would never have. Life was bliss, ignorance was bliss. I couldn't wait to meet this baby. What would they look like? How much hair would they have? My mind went crazy with possibilities and we all fell so madly in love...

We began to organise the nursery. I wanted it done before I got too big, all done so I could stick my head in and smile with excitement that soon, that room would be filled. Toys would lay on the floor, a mobile would play as he drifted off to sleep. I'd chase him as he ran from me while I tried to get him dressed. So much to look forward to.

On the 18th of December I went to the hospital when our baby stopped moving. I was taken in for an ultrasound and watched as a still baby appeared on the screen. My eyes went to our baby's chest, nothing, no flicker. In what felt like an emotional but physical pain I silently urged him to move, trying to hold back tears, please my beautiful baby, just move. Nothing. In that single moment my future changed, my family's future changed and suddenly I was empty, so incredibly empty. And holding back tears was now impossible.

On the 19th of December I arrived at the hospital to be induced. I remember the doctor giving me a tablet to put under my tongue and I just sat and stared at her, with the tablet in my hand and I cried. I knew once I took that tablet, labour would begin and my baby would be gone forever. I was in labour for eight hours and whilst the pain of contractions was awful, the emotional pain I was feeling was worse. How do we meet our baby and say goodbye in the same moment?

Our hearts were broken and we knew there wouldn't be a beautiful cry to follow all this pain. No congratulations. No smiles. And no joy at the new life wriggling in our arms. Utterly devastating. After he was born the nurse picked him up and placed him on my chest, but he didn't cry, he didn't move. I hope its the hardest moment we ever have to face in life.

He just lay there and our hearts broke again. How can I give him over to someone to take away, never to be seen again. I would never get to hold him again, never watch him grow old and never got to hear him say 'I love you Mummy'. He looked so much like his big brother. He had the most gorgeous little button nose and rosebud lips. He was amazing and beautiful.

We called him Jayden. We spent five wonderful, heartbreaking hours with him, smiling over his beauty one minute, breaking down crying the next. We wrapped him, put a beanie on his head, took photos with him and told him more times in those few hours how loved he was, more times than we possibly ever could have fitted in a lifetime.

When it was time to say our final goodbyes I placed him in the nurses arms and watched as she walked with him out the door. He was gone, for good. I would never get to see him again and I didn't know how I was supposed to move on, go forward, heal. Where do I go from here? I heard a sound and everything seemed to go black around me, when I came back around I realised that the sound had been me, a cry, a yell, a scream all in one, so painful that I had blacked out. I was literally overwhelmeed by grief.

I was wheeled back to my room and given a Pregnancy Loss Australia bear along with some other beautiful keepsakes which I now treasure. I remember sleeping with this bear on my chest that night and crying till the sun came up and still all I felt was empty. When I was told I could go home suddenly another realisation hit me, I was going home without my baby, home to a quiet house, a beautiful nursery, and all I would have were empty arms, aching just to be filled with our beautiful boy.

The church organised for us to go and stay at a holiday house for a couple of days, just to be able to get our heads around going home. But ultimately I knew I would have to face our home and nursery, and it felt incredibly daunting. When I left hospital I began to notice my milk come in and after a few hours I could barely even move my arms, they hurt so much. Every let down of milk I had I would burst into tears knowing I had nobody to feed. It was another horrible blow.

We arrived home a few days later to a quiet house. I closed Jayden's bedroom door and swore I would never go in there. But eventually, eyes full of tears, I started to pack up his room. I touched everything and every item made my cry. I grieved the fact he would never wear the little button up suit I had bought for him, would

never sleep in the cot I'd already made up, just so I could smile every time I walked past his room while he twisted and turned in my belly. I would never use the wraps all folded ready to put around his tiny wriggling frame so he felt secure and warm, nor the toys in a basket in the corner, ready for him to tip over and spread across the floor. Every item brought about so much pain, conjured so many thoughts, what-ifs and should-have-beens. As hard as it was, I allowed myself to feel it all.

The day of Jayden's funeral I felt like I was doing okay. I felt strong. I hadn't slept in nearly four weeks and I was emotionally not coping. Exacerbating my distress was the fact that my little boy that I had delivered, held, love and miss, legally, didn't exist. Because of a arbitrary law, I felt like my rights, choices and the value of my experience and loss was ignored. It seemed so cruel. So unfair. Just not right. Who had the right to undermine the life of my child, the importance of his life?

But this one day I felt okay, until I saw the tiny coffin in the back of the car at the graveside. The realisation of a funeral became very real, very confronting. How would I be able to leave him here? What if he got cold? Who would look after him if I wasn't there to?. However I remember going home that night and sleeping for twelve hours straight. I felt relief that we had honoured his short life, paid our respects and buried Jayden like any other important person would have been buried. We acknowledged his existence and his passing, because he mattered.

And then I began to dream. He was standing next to his plot and crying out 'Where is my mummy?' and it was dark and cold. I would wake up crying, wanting to jump in the car and go and get him. But I knew the reality, it was only a dream. Jayden was really gone

I started throwing all my time and energy into changing legislation about birth certificate rights for families, speaking with other families and women, and realising the enormity the effect of losing a baby has and not just on immediate family, but also how heart-breakingly common it really was. I heard horror hospital stories, and beautiful ones. I met charities and organisiations that work hard to support the substantial number of families walking the same journey and in whole, my life changed. After losing Jayden I knew I was a different me. It changes you. But now I felt like I had a purpose, his death wouldn't be for nothing. I would use it for good, for helping others who have lost, and who will lose their baby.

Because of Jayden, in South Australia, Commemorative Certificates are available through Births, Deaths and Marriages for the loss of a baby prior to 20 weeks. We hope in the not too distant future that Birth Certificates may become available, in keeping with post 20 week stillbirths. Because babies like Jayden who are stillborn, merely a few days before 20 weeks, are important too.

It has been three years since our precious boy left this world and not one day has gone by where I haven't thought about him. I still have good and bad days, the good days are starting to even up to the bad.

We have gone on to have our rainbow baby after a very rocky, anxious and scary pregnancy and he has gone some way to helping us heal, but I will never be who I was before and he will never replace our precious Jayden.

Unfortunately there seems to be a bit of a stigma towards miscarriage and stillbirth, whether it is because it involves the unborn, they just don't understand or it hurts too much for the person on the outer to think about. Know this, this time is about you and your baby. The opinions of family members, friends or strangers are unimportant unless they are aiding you on your journey towards healing and validation of your baby's existence and importance. You are allowed to grieve and in the way you see fit. If someone doesn't agree or understand, it doesn't matter. Go on how you feel, not how someone else thinks you should feel.

There is so much more to do involving research into stillbirth, and I'm hopeful, one day maybe, a link will be found and the loss of our beautiful unborn babies can be one less statistic that needs to be tallied up and the end of families walking such a painful and complex journey.

Be gentle with yourselves and know you are not alone...

Tarlia Bartsch xx

All About You...

Welcome ....

You were born on...

The time was...

The place you were born...

You were delivered by...

The people present were..

....

You weighed...

You measured...

Your head circumference was...........................

Who you looked like...

....

A Special Message for You
from Your Family

....

....

....

....

....

....

....

....

....

....

....

....

....

....

....

....

....

....

....

....

....

....

Memories to Last a Lifetime
Photos, hospital tags, pressed flowers, announcement clipping

'I held you every second of your life'
~Stephanie Paige Cole~

Memories to Last a Lifetime
Photos, hospital tags, pressed flowers, announcement clipping

'I would have given you the world, but you got heaven instead'
~Author Unknown~

My Own Words...
Poems, Journaling, Thoughts

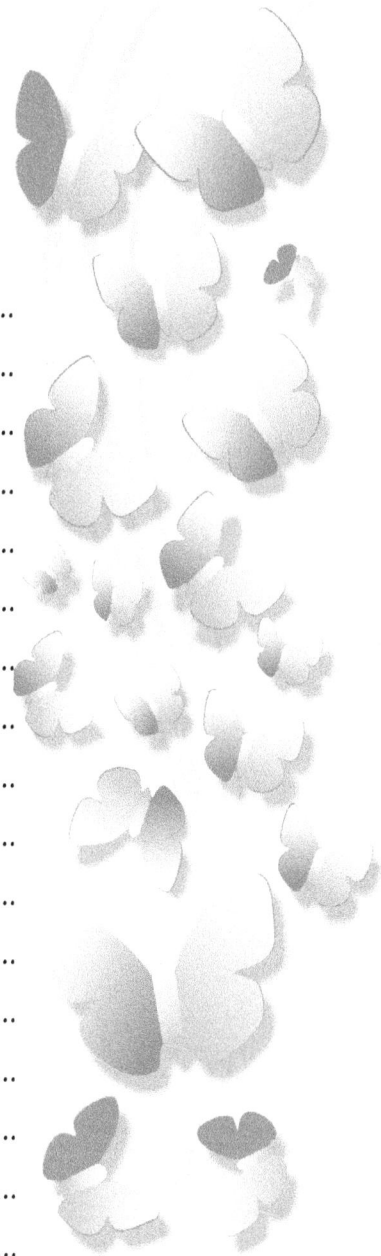

....

....

....

....

....

....

....

....

....

....

....

....

....

....

....

....

....

....

....

....

....

....

....

....

....

....

....

'What moves through us is a silence, a quiet sadness, a longing for one more day,
one more word, one more touch, we may not understand why you left his earth so soon,
or why you left before we were ready to say good-bye, but little by little,
we begin to remember not just that you died, but that you lived.
And that your life gave us... memories too beautiful to forget.'

~Author Unknown~

My Own Words...
Poems, Journaling, Thoughts

....

....

....

....

....

....

....

....

....

....

....

....

....

....

....

....

....

....

....

....

....

....

....

....

....

....

....

....

' *When a baby is born, it's a mothers instinct to protect the baby.*
When a baby dies, it's the mother's instinct to protect their memory.'

~Author Unknown~

My Own Words...
Poems, Journaling, Thoughts

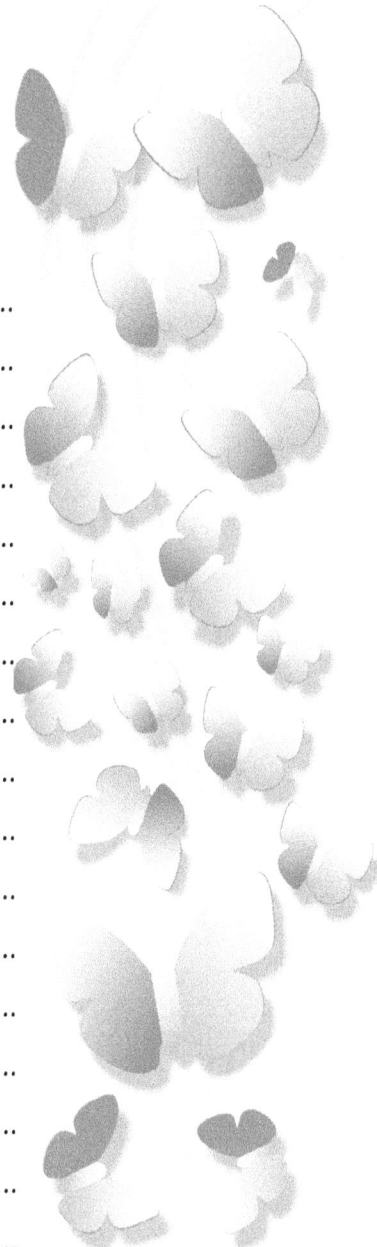

....

....

....

....

....

....

....

....

....

....

....

....

....

....

....

....

....

....

....

....

....

....

....

....

....

....

....

....

....

Footprints

'Grief is not a disease, It is not an illness, It is not depression.
It is in fact, an expression of love. Grief can only be a disease if love is.'
~Dr Joanne Cacciatore~

Handprints

'No-one wanted anything more, than I wanted you....'
~Author Unknown~

Close To My Heart...
Ultrasound pictures, belly photos

'Days will pass and turn into years....
but I'll always remember you with silent tears'
~Author Unknown~

16

Close To My Heart...
Ultrasound pictures, belly photos

'Grieving a child is like mothering a child...a life-long journey'
~Lori Spray Esteve~

Missing You

I place you in the nurse's arms,
She heads towards the door.
The world around me all goes black,
I'm broken to the core.
The silent room,
My empty arms,
My pillow stained by tears.
The questions running through my head,
Of many stolen years.
A rug to hold and snuggle dear,
A precious haunting smell.
A pain, a fear, and so much love,
For someone who's not here.

Tarlia Bartsch

A Message from Your Mum

....

....

....

....

....

....

....

....

....

....

....

....

....

....

....

....

....

....

....

....

....

....

....

....

....

....

It Must Be Very Difficult

To be a man in grief,
Since "men don't cry"
and "men are strong"
No tears can bring relief.

It must be very difficult
To stand up to the test,
And field the calls and visitors
So she can get some rest.

They always ask if she's all right
And what she's going through.
But seldom take his hand and ask,
"My friend, but how are you?"

He hears her crying in the night
And thinks his heart will break.
He dries her tears and comforts her,
But "stays strong" for her sake.

It must be very difficult
To start each day anew.
And try to be so very brave-
He lost his baby too.

~Author Unknown~

A Message from Your Dad

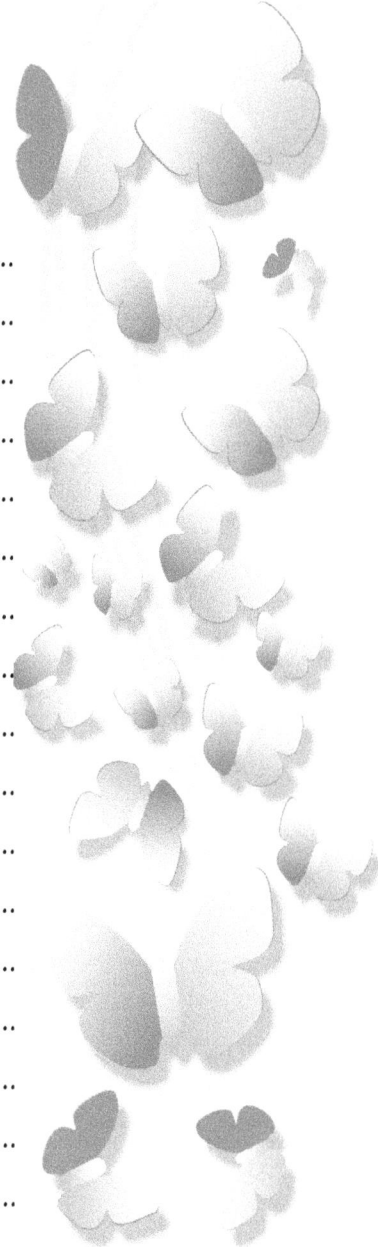

....
....
....
....
....
....
....
....
....
....
....
....
....
....
....
....
....
....
....
....
....
....
....
....
....
....
....
....

My Own Words...
Poems, Journaling, Thoughts

....

....

....

....

....

....

....

....

....

....

....

....

....

....

....

....

....

....

....

....

....

....

....

....

....

....

How We Said Goodbye

Date we said goodbye

....

What we did to celebrate you

....

....

People who came

....

....

Music we played

....

....

Flowers we brought

....

....

Scriptures/poems we read

....

....

How We Said Goodbye
funeral, cremation, memorial photos

'Some people believe in angels, I held one in my arms'
~Author Unknown~

How We Said Goodbye
funeral, cremation, memorial photos

'Some say you're too painful to remember. I say you're too precious to forget'
~Author Unknown~

Your First Anniversary

What we did to celebrate you

....

....

....

....

How we felt

....

....

....

....

Who came

....

....

....

....

Your Second Anniversary

What we did to celebrate you

....

....

....

....

How we felt

....

....

....

....

Who came

....

....

....

....

Your Third Anniversary

What we did to celebrate you

....

....

....

....

How we felt

....

....

....

....

Who came

....

....

....

....

Your Fourth Anniversary

What we did to celebrate you

....

....

....

....

How we felt

....

....

....

....

Who came

....

....

....

....

Your Fifth Anniversary

What we did to celebrate you

....

....

....

....

How we felt

....

....

....

....

Who came

....

....

....

....

Support Organisations Available
Australia

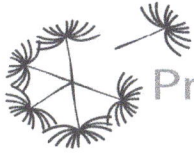

Pregnancy Loss Australia

(formerly known as Teddy Love Club) is a national support program for bereaved families who suffer the loss of their baby or babies from miscarriage, stillbirth, termination for abnormality and neo-natal loss through our early support program and professional support services.

www.pregnancylossaustralia.org.au
contactus@pregnancylossaustralia.org.au
General Phone: 1300 720 942
Support Phone: 1800 824 240

At SIDS and Kids South Australia

we are dedicated to saving the lives of babies and children during pregnancy, birth, infancy and childhood and supporting bereaved families. We provide a 24 hour, 365 days a year crisis outreach service as well as ongoing bereavement support for families following the sudden and unexpected death of an infant or young child from conception to 6 years. We also provide safe sleeping education to the South Australian community in an effort to prevent sleeping accidents.

24 Hour Bereavement Support Line: 1300 308 307   Office: (08) 8369 0155

The Chance's Clothes Project

provides hospitals with Baby Bereavement Clothing packages free of charge for distribution to parents who have experienced the tragedy of miscarriage or stillbirth of their baby.
We seek the talent and generosity of volunteers to knit, sew and crochet Baby Bereavement Clothing for our packages. Join our team and help us wrap all angel babies with love.
Email: chances.clothes@yahoo.com.au
Website: www.chancesclothesproject.com

Support Organisations Available
Australia

Karen is an experienced and compassionate qualified Counsellor Consultant, who has an interest and passion around bereavement and grief which started at the age of 12. She has worked in a number of community based services and is a contracted counsellor for Pregnancy Loss Australia, nationwide. Along with Karen's training in generic counselling, bereavement and grief, Karen also brings much insight and knowledge from her life experiences and relationship with her own, unique grieving process and the skills she has to journey through the pain of loss, which in turn supports her work as she companions others when invited to do so.
Support services are available Australia and New Zealand wide.
www.karenjefferson.com
karenjeffersoncounsellor@gmail.com

Heartfelt is a volunteer organisation of professional photographers from all over Australia, dedicated to giving the gift of photographic memories to families that have experienced stillbirths, premature births, or have children with serious and terminal illnesses.

Heartfelt is dedicated to providing this gift to families in a caring, compassionate manner. All services are free of charge.
For a full contact list of state representatives visit:
www.heartfelt.org.au
or call 1800 583 768

Happy Castings - Specialising in Angel Babies, Intensive Care Units and The Terminally Ill only. A Treasured Keepsake of your Baby or Child's Hands and Feet with or without a photo, beautifully framed to cherish forever.
Servicing South Australia.

Happy Castings, PO Box 376, Woodside SA 5244
Phone: 0432 090 818
Email: enquiries@happycastings.com.au

Support Organisations Available
Australia

NICU Helping Hands Angel Gown Program. From donated wedding gowns we lovingly hand craft Angel Gown garments which are then gifted to Neonatal Intensive Care Units, and Hospitals all around Australia, for babies who are born sleeping or grow their wings far too soon. We also make to order for any family who wants to wrap their baby or young child in the love of their own wedding gown.
www.angelgownprogram.org.au

Sands are a self-help support organisation: where trained volunteers (who are all parents whose expected baby has died) offer peer support to other bereaved parents and their families.
Sharing with others who have had similar experiences can assist parents to work through the often intense grief which follows the death of a baby.
There are active Sands groups in most states.
Support is available by phone (1300 0 sands; 1300 0 72637) online at www.sands.org.au and through social media.

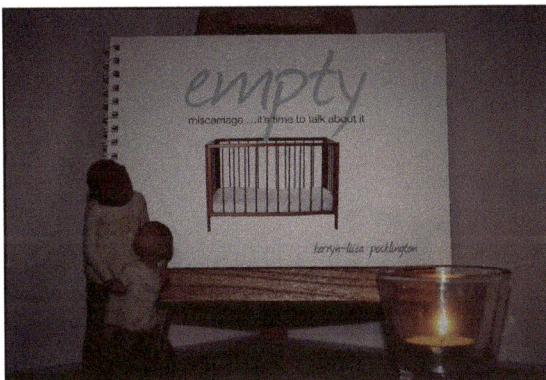

Empty - Miscarriage Journal - A source of hope and comfort for those experiencing baby loss, and a great gift when you don't know the words to say.
Contact details: empty_author@hotmail.com
www.facebook.com/empty.miscarriage
Available Australia wide and Internationally directly from author.

Support Organisations Available

nilmdts
Now I Lay Me Down to Sleep

Now I Lay Me Down to Sleep is a USA based charity which provides remembrance photography to parents suffering the loss of a baby, with a free gift of professional portraiture. NILMDTS trains, educates, and mobilises professional quality photographers to provide beautiful heirloom portraits to families facing the untimely death of an infant. We believe these images serve as an important step in the family's healing process by honouring the child's legacy.
www.nowilaymedowntosleep.org

Research and Prevention

Stillbirth Foundation
AUSTRALIA
Research and Education to Prevent Stillbirth

The Stillbirth Foundation Australia's mission is to help reduce the high incidence of stillbirth through research, education and advocacy.

For more information visit:
www.stillbirthfoundation.org.au
Email: office@stillbirthfoundation.org.au

COUNT THE KICKS
empowering mums-to-be with knowledge & confidence

www.countthekicks.org.uk

Count The Kicks is a UK pregnancy charity that educates mums-to-be on baby movements with the aim of ensuring the healthy delivery of babies who may be struggling in the womb.
Area of support:
UK for literature, enquiries welcomed worldwide.

"For you created my inmost being;
you knit me together in my mother's womb.
I praise you because I am fearfully and wonderfully made;
your works are wonderful, I know that full well.
My frame was not hidden from you when I was made in the secret place,
when I was woven together in the depths of the earth.
Your eyes saw my unformed body;
all the days ordained for me were written
in your book before one of them came to be."

~Psalm 139: 13-16~

Photos of you...

'In our arms for a little while, in our hearts forever.'
~Author Unknown~

Photos of you...

'Breathe. Listen for my footfall in your heart. I am not gone but merely walk within you.'
~Nicholas Evans~

One Last Kiss

I wrap your tiny body,
And hold you tightly near.
I kiss your precious forehead,
And whisper sweetly in your ear.
I say how much I love you,
And that I can't let go.
I want to take you home with us,
For the whole world to show.
I want to hear you cry,
To wipe away your tears.
To kiss away your booboos,
And hug away your fears.
To tuck you in to bed at night,
To dress you up for school.
To watch you drive your first car,
Or watch you say 'I do'.
I hold your tiny dear frame,
And think of all I'll miss.
I say Goodbye and I Love You,
And give you one last kiss.

Tarlia Bartsch

My Own Words...
Poems, Journaling, Thoughts

....

....

....

....

....

....

....

....

....

....

....

....

....

....

....

....

....

....

....

....

....

....

....

....

....

....

....

....

Photos of you...

'If love could have saved you, you would have lived forever.'
~Author Unknown~

Photos of you...

'If every tear we shed for you became a star above, you'd stroll in Angel's garden, lit by everlasting love.'
~Author Unknown~

Four Precious Girls...

We wrap you up our precious girls and take you in our arms,
The tears stream freely down our face, your beauty clearly charms.
We touch your precious feet and toes, spy your delicate small frames,
We look in to your tiny face, and whisper your beautiful names.
We kiss you on your button nose, and smile as we cry,
Such awe at your beauty, such pain at your short lives.
We wrap you oh so gently, place a beanie on your heads,
The life we face with out you all, our heart....... it simply dreads.
Your pictures on the mantle piece, your ashes side by side,
Never in our long lives, your existence will we hide.
You came, you lived, and our love for you it oozes from our core.
Of nothing will we ever be, so clearly, totally sure.
Please know we miss you precious girls, our lives wont be the same,
And at every single chance we get, we will proudly speak your name.

Tarlia Bartsch

For Shelley and Rick
In Memory of their precious girls
Matilda, Pearl, Mabel and Elsa

Gone, but remembered and loved by many.....

My Own Words...
Poems, Journaling, Thoughts

....

....

....

....

....

....

....

....

....

....

....

....

....

....

....

....

....

....

....

....

....

....

....

....

....

....

....

....

....

A Place to Visit You...

I never got to see your face,
Hear you laugh or start to cry.
I never got to kiss your cheeks
Or whisper a last a goodbye.

You were whisked away,
to an unnamed place,
I was left with much unknown.
And the thoughts about a lifetime gone,
It broke me to the bone.

Where have you gone my sweet, sweet baby?
Where do you finally lay?
I silently dream about so much,
Each and every aching day.

This pain it always lingers,
And the tears are just below.
I try so hard to bury it,
So my heartbreak doesn't show.

Were you a boy or a little girl?
Are answers I may never get.
But no matter how many years that pass,
Your birth I will never forget.

As I sit down now,
And stare into space,
And tears they fill my eyes
I have a place to finally visit you,
And every other baby that dies.

Tarlia Bartsch

~Dedicated to all those families who never got the choice to say hello or goodbye and read at the opening of the Baby Remembrance Garden in Port Lincoln on the 3rd of August, 2014~

My Own Words...
Poems, Journaling, Thoughts

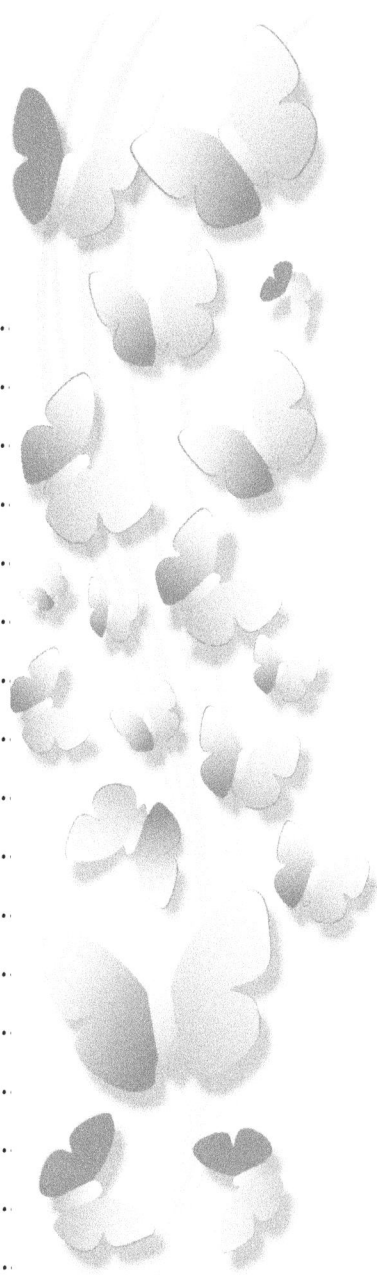

Thank you

To the amazing men in my life Lukas, Marco and Jaxon, thank you for just being you.
For everyday giving me a reason to wake up, for the laughs, the tears and for the days I want to
pull my hair out! I love you all so much and want to reflect this in everything I do for you!

To our family, Thank you! You have walked through this journey with us, you have felt
what we've felt and been our strength. Thank you for honouring Jaydens memory and life in
anyway you can and your incredible support.

To Pastor Rob and Pauline and my church family, thank you so much for your support,
your prayers and meals. You show a true christian heart, compassion, giving,
gentle guidance and .....just plain love!

To all the wonderful people that helped make this book happen,
in many different ways, thank you!
There are far too many of you to name individually,
but I appreciate everyone of you!

To the families I have met on this journey of pain, confusion,
questions and guilt, our babies have brought us together. I feel
blessed to have met you all and although I wish it was under better
circumstances, it has given us a little bit of help to know that we
are not alone. I truly pray for peace and healing for you all as
we all learn to live with a big piece of our hearts missing.

Jayden, everyday is a new day faced with out you. The thought of
all the things we have missed seeing you do, hearing you say and enjoying
with you is incredibly heartbreaking and confronting.
Not a day goes by that we don't think of you or speak your name.
We wish we could hold you in our arms again and admire your
beautiful face, touch your toes and play with your fingers. You
have given me a new lease on life...
'Live life to the fullest, enjoy every moment, hold dear to
what's important and let go of what's not...
but most importantly life is precious, short and not promised.'

Rest in peace our beautiful boy and know you are so incredibly loved by so many!

Especially Mum, Dad, Marco and Jaxon. xxx

I'll See You Again One Day...

I often lay awake at night,
and day dream of your face.
I still cant seem to grasp the fact
You are in a 'better' place.
I want you here and in my arms
to kiss and hug and hold.
To watch you grow and learn and play
Until I am too old.
Instead I'm left with emptiness,
A pain that lingers near.
And thoughts about your tiny voice,
my ears will never hear.
What age would you have stood up straight
and walked into my arms,
What word would you have yelled out loud,
With such eagerness and charm.
What would have been your favourite toy
or food or way to sleep.
Would you have been real peaceful,
or happy to make a peep.
These questions, wants, desires
will forever haunt my mind.
And days that I don't cry for you
are very hard to find.
Just know we miss you baby boy
in our thoughts you're not far away
And I get a touch peace to know,
Ill see your face again one day.

Tarlia Bartsch

www.ingramcontent.com/pod-product-compliance
Lightning Source LLC
Chambersburg PA
CBHW040858100426
42813CB00015B/2836